Praise for God

M000101352

"I am excited about Mark's new book entitled ***God's Craftsman***. I love Mark's commonsense approach to bringing forth these life-changing principles, and his track record proves an incredible wisdom in business and ministry. You won't ever look at your future the same way again once you have read this book."

Edward J Windsor
Senior Pastor–Champion Life Church, Palm Desert, CA

"If you desire to reach a higher level in your work or in life this book will give you practical steps how to get there."

Dr. Bob Harrison
America's Increase Authority

"God's Craftsmen is a book for every person who longs to tie together their purpose on earth in light of their vocation."

Phil Hotsenpiller
Senior Pastor–Influence Church, Anahein, CA

"Mark Chapman is a man of great credibility, integrity and influence. This book will challenge you, inspire you, and equip you to steward your call to work in a more intentional and effective way."

Lyle Wells
President–Integrus Leadership

GOD'S CRAFTSMAN

Embracing Your Call to Work

MARK CHAPMAN

26 25 24 23 22 21   9 8 7 6 5 4 3 2 1

GOD'S CRAFTSMAN
Copyright ©2021 Mark Chapman

Author Website: www.godscraftsman.org

Published by:
Emerge Publishing, LLC
2109 East 69th Street Tulsa, OK 74136
Phone: 888.407.4447 www.Emerge.pub

Library of Congress Cataloging-in-Publication Data:
ISBN: 978-1-954966-16-1 Paperback
E-book available exclusively on Kindle

BISAC:
SEL027000 SELF-HELP / Personal Growth / Success
BUS107000 BUSINESS & ECONOMICS / Personal Success
BUS019000 BUSINESS & ECONOMICS / Decision-Making & Problem Solving

Printed in the United States of America

CONTENTS

This book is dedicated to all who are searching for meaning in their daily work.

FOREWORD

Your work can be an act of worship to God. This happens when you dedicate your work to God and perform it as an offering to Him. All of life, including work, should be considered sacred—especially when you put your heart and soul into what you're doing.

Unfortunately, many Christians hold an incorrect view of work. They have a false distinction between what they perceive as sacred (prayer, ministry, church attendance, etc.) and secular (work, along with basically anything outside of church). This sacred-secular dichotomy makes people believe that pastors are spiritual, but businessmen and businesswomen are not. Prayer is spiritual, but work is not. Sadly, this kind of thinking compartmentalizes our lives and keeps us from being effective where God has placed us—which, for the most of us, is outside the confines of the church!

Over the years, here's what I've discovered: Each one of us were born on purpose, for a purpose. We all have a gift or gifts that have been entrusted to us by God. These unique gifts on our life complement our callings and enable us to function effectively in them. When we function in our God-given gifts and abilities, our hearts are awakened, and we are infused with strength and vigor. In those instances, hours of work can seem like only minutes! Regardless of how you view yourself and your giftings, you'll never be truly satisfied in life until you fully embrace the work you've been given to do and invest yourself into that.

Your gift, whether it operates best in healthcare, education, government, athletics, the marketplace, the arts, the media, the home, or any other arena, has a connection to building the kingdom. God designed it this way! In this timely book, *God's Craftsman*, my friend Mark will help you to connect your dots so you can understand the significance of both your calling and your gifts and how they are pivotal for you to make your life count, both now and for eternity.

Work is a gift from God. So are your unique talents and abilities. When you put them to work, it's your gift back to God.

John Bevere
Best-selling Author and Minister
Co-founder of Messenger International and MessengerX.com

INTRODUCTION

The amazing thing about the Bible is that it was written over several millennia and penned centuries ago, yet it still complements itself and holds timeless truths. While many people view the Bible as a religious book only, it is very much a book for all aspects of life. It is still relevant today. You can find answers and principles that apply to every topic, including your daily work.

You've probably heard from a minister or elsewhere the phrase, "God has a plan and a purpose for your life." Or, "He created you for something special." Yet what does that mean to those of us who are accountants, painters, truck drivers, salespeople, or _____ fill in the blank. Is there really a purpose to that job or task? Why do we work? What is it really about?

As I meet various people through business or church or with friends, I often hear others share struggles similar to my own. I found out that I am not alone. We are all on a similar journey. So, the reason I wrote this book is to share with you the thoughts and processes that I went through to reach a place of true fulfillment in my vocation and how that change in perspective has carried over into other areas of my life. I reached a place of knowing I am in the center of where God wants me to be. When you embrace the truths and principles I've learned in this book, you will find that your life becomes more purposeful. Your work becomes more meaningful and satisfying. And you will achieve a higher level of success. That shift has been truly liberating and life changing.

WHY do we work?

Most Americans spend 40 to 50 hours per week at their jobs or work-related activities. Multiply that by 50 weeks a year, and that is well over 2,000 hours spent working or on associated tasks. Contrast that to perhaps two to five hours a week at church, community group, or other church-related activities. Even taking five hours a week multiplied by 52 weeks a year, that's only a little more than 250 hours. This means you spend nearly ten times as much time at your job, career, or vocation as you do at church. On one hand, this may seem way out of balance, yet we all know we must work. We have to make a living and provide for ourselves and our families. Even God worked six days. So how do we translate this into meaningful activity, productivity, and purpose? Does this mean that we should work half as much and go to church twice as much? I don't think so. When God created Adam, he gave him the garden to take care of. Obviously, God wanted him to "work." God did not say go to church four hours every day. The children of Israel were certainly God's holy people, and so are we. But he didn't expect them to sit around singing hallelujahs all day long.

When I was a child, we went to church Sunday morning, Sunday night, and Wednesday night with another activity or two usually sprinkled in between. Perhaps we need to get back to some form or fashion of that schedule. Regularly being in the House of God is essential.

Nevertheless, we as humans always have, and will continue to, spend the bulk of our time outside the church walls. A large portion of that time is spent on the job. So, what does God want us to do with that time?

Further study of Scripture reveals quite a bit about work and marketplace ministry. So many times, we have placed such an emphasis on ministry (usually meaning five-fold ministry) that we tend to think work is just this outside activity that we must trudge through or that the two never overlap. Quite the contrary—I am more convinced than ever, and I wish I had learned this more thoroughly earlier in my career, that work is indeed a calling and a ministry.

The good news is that as I studied the Bible through the vantage point of my vocation and I began to work through the principles I share in this book, I had a profound shift in my thinking and how I approached my business and career. This brought about an increase in my income, expanded my business and ministry opportunities, and increased my level of fulfillment and career satisfaction.

So often, famous people and heroes of the Bible get all the attention. Ministers from the pulpit talk about and emphasize "working in" or being "called to" the ministry. Yet there are many, many examples in Scripture of simple people, lay people, ordinary people doing their jobs and doing them as a work unto the Lord, playing a vital role in God's plan. That is the purpose of this book: That you come to a place where you do not view your job or vocation or career as just something to get a paycheck. That you work for meaning and not just money. I hope you learn to see your work as a way that the Lord can use you and move through you and that your work has a definite purpose in the kingdom of God. That you have a marketplace ministry.

How many of you have ever heard of Bezalel? (More on him later.) Has anyone ever preached a sermon about him? Perhaps, but I have not ever heard it. Yet God appointed him and called him for a specific purpose. He didn't write the Bible, he wasn't a prophet, he wasn't a warrior. He was a skilled craftsman called to do a particular task and use his talent for God's purpose. That's the point!

This book is meant to help you find meaning in your work. I hope by the time you are finished reading this you will see your daily activities, your work, your vocation, and your unique talent and competency as gifts from God to be used Monday through Friday, to accomplish great things, maximize your potential, have a fulfilling life, bless other people, and bring him glory.

CHAPTER 1

MY JOURNEY

Many of us have struggled at some point in our lives with meaning and purpose, why we are here, and/or what do we do for a living. It is a common theme of sermons and books and a common topic among nearly all of us who work. I find it especially true among men. But sometimes, as we pursue our work, this concept seems so elusive.

Granted, we've all taken jobs or had positions where we needed the income, particularly early in our working careers as kids or young adults. I don't think any child says, "When I grow up, I want to wash dishes at a restaurant." I did it for six months when

I was 15. I hated it. But I liked having a paycheck. The Bible says a person who doesn't work shouldn't eat. So, we have to work to provide and pay for our obligations. But seemingly, as we get older and mature, many of us struggle with the "why" of work. I wrestled with it for a good portion of my life.

I was raised in the church. While I am grateful for a biblical Christian foundation, no one actually taught me how to truly live my life. It felt like it was simply "fire insurance": be good, obey God, get saved, or you'll go to hell; don't screw up during the week or you're going to have to come to the altar again on Sunday. Meanwhile, life Monday through Saturday wasn't that great in many ways. As I grew older, I searched for meaning and purpose—I began digging deeper into the Bible and into other philosophies of life. I was searching for meaning. What did I truly believe? What was the truth? Did I go to church simply because I was told to or because that's how I was raised? Or did I believe the Bible was true and the gospel message was The Way? I concluded that the Bible is indeed true, and Jesus Christ truly became my Lord and Savior.

Now what do I do???

It seemed all the emphasis was on "go make disciples," on telling others with the implicit meaning that you had to "be in the ministry." To be sure, we as Christians are to indeed be a witness to all those we may encounter. Maybe I just missed it, but I never really heard much about ministry Monday through Friday or what my work life was all about. Work was simply something we all did to make money, pay the bills, and pay our tithes. But God forbid you made too much money or you might become corrupt. It seemed like so many mixed messages: we go to church, praise God, and then we gripe and moan about our jobs. I have been guilty of this. Yet somehow, deep inside, I felt a call to do something special for God. Like most believers, I wanted to please him. "Lord, what do you want me to do with my life?" So many of us have prayed that prayer and seemingly come up empty. You may have even felt guilty about having a desire to do a particular thing, task, endeavor, or career because it wasn't "spiritual enough."

I struggled with this for many years—a seeming tug of war between doing something for God versus providing for my family and making a living, working to pay the bills, so on and so on.

Some people seem to know from an early age what they want to do in life and set out on a more focused career pathway. I have a very good friend who, as a young boy, became enamored with home construction. At about age ten or so, a new housing development started near his neighborhood. He suddenly was fascinated with the framed houses and the construction process. He would wander over there and explore and learn. He would then go home and draw and design houses. He knew as he grew older, he wanted to build and design things, and he went to the University of Michigan to study architecture. He worked in construction and ultimately went on to earn his degree in architecture. Right out of college, he began working for a builder as a laborer and worked his way up. Today he is vice president of a major home building company. He loves what he does, is very good at it, and always knew that's what he wanted to do. Me, not so much. I wasn't one of those people. My interests were wide and varied.

As a young man, I felt something of a "call to ministry," but nothing seemed quite right. I didn't want to go to Bible school or study theology. I was fairly certain I didn't want to do weddings and funerals. I didn't consider myself to have the gift of evangelism. However, I wanted my life to mean something for the kingdom of God. I wanted to please my Savior.

I grew up in a small town in Iowa. I have some very fond memories, but it wasn't always great. I don't want to make excuses, but I had some disadvantages to overcome and work through. I was an only child. My mother was a single mom, living on welfare and the good deeds of those in our local church. She also suffered from mental illness. At times, it was severe. She could not hold a job, and she didn't even know how to drive. And although many good and caring people helped us out, I had few strong examples of Christian manhood or, more specifically, of a career-minded person or someone motivated for success.

I share these things not to say, "Woe was me," but to illustrate that I came from very modest beginnings, with no actual knowledge or instruction on how to build a successful career or successful, productive life. No one encouraged me to pursue my dreams. I didn't know how or even know it was possible. Yet today, I have a very good life and a successful business. If it can happen to me, it can happen to you.

As I grew a little older, I was somewhat of a confused and troubled teenager headed in the wrong direction. Fortunately, when I was 16, I went to a youth camp and truly had a salvation experience. I had planned to visit my dad that summer in Oklahoma and went ahead with that trip. Somehow during that summer, by God's grace, I knew in my heart that if I went back to Iowa and my old way of life, I would probably struggle. So I moved to Tulsa, Oklahoma, to live with my father and stepfamily. As I enrolled in a new high school and selected courses, I picked a vocational course in electronics. This was a little bit by luck, but it was probably God, and I just didn't know it. I kind of liked it and seemed to have a knack for it. I understood it. This ultimately landed me a full-ride scholarship to Oklahoma State Tech, a very good technical school. I quickly got my associate degree and went to work. This launched me on a path where this knowledge would ultimately help me. Yet after a few short years, I didn't feel that being a technician was what I wanted to do.

I did a variety of things in my 20s and 30s. I always prayed about the next move to make or what job to take or not take. I probably applied for some jobs or tried things that were not wise or the best fit. And in hindsight, I don't know that I missed God on my job selection. Yet oftentimes, I was definitely unfulfilled. When I was in my mid-20s, my father-in-law started a company producing and selling children's Bible story videos and books. It was not a ministry; it was a for-profit business. I decided to help him and went to work for this new company. This was a great thing in my mind because we were providing a tool to reach kids with the gospel, and I still could have fun in business. I felt our business had a definite purpose. And hopefully, we would make some money. What I came to realize during my time there is that I had a desire to make a good living or an above-average income so that I could share it and have more opportunities both personally and for church-related work. And that's not wrong! (More on this to come.)

After a few years of working for that company, what I also began to realize was that I did indeed enjoy the business side of what I was doing: purchasing, accounting, hiring, marketing. It being a small enterprise, I wore several hats. I had the title general manager. I don't remember if I gave that title to myself, but I did have a hand in most areas of the business. In my early 30s, to improve my skills and increase my hiring opportunities, I went back to school part-time and completed a bachelor's degree in management. Unfortunately, the business was not very financially successful. But I learned a lot, and I learned that I did enjoy the business world. There was also a desire growing in me to be my own boss and to have my own company. I just didn't know what kind of company. After about ten years and having kids in the house to feed, I realized it was time for a change.

I stumbled across a position in sales with a company selling professional video equipment. My father built some cabinets for their office. One day as I told him I was ready to make a job change, my dad mentioned this company and suggested I check them out. I made a call, and one of their salespeople had just left, so they had an opening. I investigated it, and I got an offer. Actually, I didn't stumble across this job ... I believe God led me there. At the same time, I had also applied for a job as an underwriter trainee with State Farm Insurance. It wasn't so much that I wanted to be an underwriter, but I knew State Farm had benefits and various career paths that I could pursue. The other job was commission-oriented and a small company. Both offers came in at virtually the same time. Now I had a choice to make: What do I do? What's going to fulfill me, and what's going to provide for my family? After much prayer, I declined State Farm even though I felt it was more secure. But inside, I felt like it genuinely wouldn't satisfy me and would not pay as well in the long run. We all know that money isn't everything, but YES, I factored in the income potential too. I took a chance.

Come to find out, I was pretty good at the sales job. It started out very well, and I was enjoying my time … I had a successful run at this company. So as I look back and think about it now, I "just happened" to pick the electronics courses in high school. I could have easily done auto mechanics or woodworking. Excelling in that, I got my two-year education paid for, which led to some good technical jobs in my early twenties. This technical aptitude came in handy when I went to work for my father-in-law. I was programming computers and making decisions on software systems and PCs to buy. I got involved with producing TV commercials and in the production and editing of the children's videos we sold. I worked with TV stations, and I was around video production and editing gear. I also began to learn accounting. But we had to market these video products too, so I worked on my sales and marketing skills. Then, my dad "just happened" to mention this company he built the cabinets for. And they had just lost a salesperson when I called. When I got the opportunity to sell video equipment, I had something of a foundation to start from, having the electronics degree and the video work I did at the previous position. While it was primarily a sales position, I continued to learn more about running a business. I had tremendous favor at this company and grew a lot, both in practical and spiritual ways. I had a decent lifestyle for a number of years. Despite the perceived highs and lows, my time in this position was definitely beneficial in helping me get to where I am today.

But I began to grow restless and dissatisfied. That desire to be my own boss continued to grow—a desire to run an organization, set the direction, organize, be in charge and make decisions or call the shots. At a minimum, I wanted to at least find something more fulfilling. I was continually investigating job opportunities, trying to figure out what I should do. Then the company I worked for began to struggle. The owners were good people. Unfortunately, as the years went on, the business developed some problems. It was getting harder for me to stay. Suddenly, it seemed like a light bulb went on in my head, or maybe it was God's voice. "Mark, you are pretty good at this job. Why do you keep fighting it?" But I pondered this thought very carefully. I realized that of all the things I had tried, selling professional video gear was what I'd had the most success at. After much prayer and counsel, I approached my boss and told him I would be leaving and the reasons why. I explained why I was dissatisfied and tried to be fair to him. He replied to me, "You may have an itch that I cannot scratch." And you know what, I think he was absolutely right. He was gracious to me upon my departure.

Even though I wasn't a huge risk-taker, and it seemed to take a while, after more than a decade after being in this business, I finally made the decision to start my own company. Maybe I should have done it sooner, or maybe I wasn't ready. Maybe I was just in the wrong environment. Maybe it took me that long to truly understand myself. Perhaps I'm a late bloomer. Or maybe it was simply God's timing. There is always a season of preparation in our lives for the next endeavor. That can be weeks, months, or even years. Whatever the reasons, looking back from where I'm at today, I can see how every step of my path, the zigs and zags ... the times where there were problems or challenges ... or dissatisfaction... the biblical business principles I've learned ... the choices I made ... all helped me achieve the success I now have.

As I was on this journey of trying to figure out what I wanted to do, I still tried to maintain a good attitude and find meaning and purpose in whatever I was doing at the time. I wasn't always perfect at it, but my prayer was:

"Lord, help me to have a good attitude.
Lord, help my light shine while I work.
Lord, help me do the best job I can do.
Lord, show me how to honor my boss.
Lord, help me use my talent and my income to help my church and other people."

As I said, there were days where I didn't exactly fulfill these prayers. But I was giving it my best effort. This should be your prayer or your posture too, no matter where you are in your work life, either just starting out or at the end of your career.

All along the way, in my 20s and 30s, I applied for a variety of jobs. I dabbled in some self-employment opportunities. I read books and took tests on personality profiles and skills assessments. While I always learned something, it still felt a little futile. But I think the reason why is because I was always trying to be somebody else instead of being me. I wasn't willing to connect the dots, be honest with myself, and just say, "Hey, I want to earn some money and run a small business. So what if the next guy is an engineer or corporate VP or high up in a sales organization or an airplane pilot?" Wow, those things sound intriguing and cool! But it wasn't in my heart of hearts, and it wasn't in my personality. Maybe you've heard the phrase "being comfortable in your own skin." It took me a while to get there.

But I finally came to the place where I understood myself and what I wanted, and I embraced how God created me. I came to the place where I could find purpose, meaning, and joy in my work. I now view my work and my career totally as a call from God. He has equipped me to be his craftsman in my specific field of work.

After you read this book, I hope it doesn't take you nearly as long to embrace your career calling as it did for me. Figure out who you are or what you want to do, and then go for it. Maximize it. Maximize yourself to your full potential. Take joy in it! Stop the comparison game!

So now you've heard my story. What is yours? Maybe you are now, and have been, exactly on course for what you want and need to do in your work and career. But if not, are you ready to restart and reset? Are you ready to be God's craftsman? Are you ready to be his specialist, his worker, his instrument for a specific task or duty? Are you ready to find meaning and fulfillment and understand your purpose in your vocation, and then succeed in it? Then let's get started!

I now view my work and my career totally as a call from God. He has equipped me to be his craftsman in my specific field of work.

CHAPTER 2

WORK IS MINISTRY

What is your first reaction to the title of this chapter? Does it strike you as an odd statement? Or perhaps you've already settled that question in your heart. What does it mean that work is ministry?

For years, I never really thought of my daily routine in this way. And I don't recall hearing much Bible teaching about it. One day, after many years of working, it dawned on me that my work was not just for myself. A thought hit me, and I have been tempted to say that work or a worker is a "sixth fold" ministry. Please don't misunderstand my intent: I'm not creating a doctrine nor do I want to get into trouble with theologians and people far more schooled in the Bible than I am. The New Testament does teach about the five-fold ministry very clearly (Ephesians 4), and those ministry gifts have obvious importance. However, most of us are not in those capacities. Most of us simply "work" at a "job." Therefore, we should understand and discover that we all have a gift for some form of work. That is why I say work is a ministry. I believe your work is MEANT to bring you joy, to serve others, to serve God, and to bring him glory. You are called to be salt and light in the marketplace.

The Bible puts it this way:

"Whatever you do, do your work heartily, as for the Lord and not for people" (Colossians 3:23 NASB).

> I believe your work is MEANT to bring you joy, to serve others, to serve God, and to bring him glory. You are called to be salt and light in the marketplace.

"'Your light must shine before people in such a way that they may see your good works and glorify your Father, who is in heaven'" (Matthew 5:16 NASB).

That word *work* in Matthew 5:16 is the Greek word "ergon." According to Strong's Concordance, it means just that: "work." Its usage includes task, employment, deed, action, or that which is wrought or made. I dug a little further, and Strong's Word Studies says "*érgon* (from *ergō*, 'to work, accomplish')

— a *work* or *worker* who accomplishes something." Continuing on, Strong's Reference 2041 says: *"lérgon* («work») is a deed (action) that carries out (completes) <u>an inner desire</u> (intension, purpose)."

So, if we say that in reverse, your work should complete an inner desire and be an action that brings God glory.

As the children of Israel were leaving Egypt, they came to Mount Sinai, and Moses received the Ten Commandments from the Lord. The fourth commandant says this:

"For six days work may be done, but on the seventh day, there is a Sabbath of complete rest, holy to the Lord" (Exodus 31:15 NASB).

The main point of this verse is really about honoring the Sabbath. However, God obviously knew that people would work. <u>Without work, there would be no need for a Sabbath</u>. God fully expected his people to create, build, and engage in commerce and provide for their needs.

In Malachi 3:10, God says to bring the tithe into the storehouse. And Proverbs 3:9 (NIV) says, "Honor the Lord with your wealth, / with the firstfruits of all your crops, your produce or increase." How can you obey these Scriptures if you do not work? Does it not make sense that work and productivity come before the tithe and the firstfruits?

According to Bible Gateway, an online search states that there are well over 25 occupations and industries referenced in the Bible, which is probably a conservative estimate. I want to establish that work is very much a part of God's plan and a key part of our Christian walk.

The following are several examples of people in the Bible who were identified simply as workers, people with jobs and skills, or as we would say now, they had vocations, professions, or careers.

Abel was a shepherd. Cain was a farmer. (Genesis 4:2)

Abram was rich in livestock, gold, and silver. He must have been a shrewd businessman. (Genesis 13:2)

Joseph was a skilled manager and organizer. (Genesis 41)

Bezalel was skilled in all kinds of craftsmanship. (Exodus 31)

David raised sheep and was a musician. He was a great military man. (1 Samuel)

Many craftsmen are mentioned during the building of the tabernacle and the temple. (Exodus 31, 35; 2 Chronicles)

Merchants and traders (businesspeople) are referenced in Solomon's efforts to build the temple. (1 Kings 10:14-15, 28-29; 2 Chronicles 1:16-17)

Nehemiah recounts the names of dozens of people who helped rebuild the wall. (Nehemiah 3)

The Old Testament frequently mentions craftsmen, artisans, masons, potters, blacksmiths, goldsmiths, etc.

Peter, James, and John were fishermen. (Luke 5)

Matthew was a tax collector, an unpopular duty, but it obviously required some skill in math and record-keeping as well as other areas of expertise. (Matthew 9:9)

Luke was a physician. (Colossians 4:14)

Paul was a tentmaker, as were Acquila and Priscilla. (Acts 18:3)

Lydia, a woman, was a seller of an exceptionally fine purple dye and ministered to the apostles. (Acts 16:14)

Zenas, apparently a close friend of Paul's, was a lawyer. (Titus 3:13)

While we don't know exactly what they did, it's obvious the subjects in the parable of the talents were in the marketplace because they multiplied what they were given through work, trade, or exchange. (Matthew 25:14-30)

> My hunch is that Jesus was very good at what he did and was probably known for it. His work was not shoddy. He was a craftsman.

And of course, Jesus is commonly thought of as being a carpenter before He began his ministry. There is some school of thought that says perhaps He was a stone mason.

In fact, according to Robby Galatty:

> "The central misunderstanding comes from a translation issue that occurred centuries ago. It focuses on a verse in Matthew 13. After Jesus teaches in his hometown synagogue, the crowd asks, "Is not this the carpenter's son? Is not his mother called Mary?" (v. 55). The Greek word *tekton,* translated here as carpenter, is more accurately rendered as **craftsman** or builder" [emphasis added]. [1]

Another thought I found interesting is that some speculate this could be why Jesus referred to himself as the "chief cornerstone." I don't want to split hairs over what Jesus did for a living. The point is that even Jesus had a career before launching into ministry. Whether carpenter or stone mason, my hunch is that Jesus was very good at what he did and was probably known for it. His work was not shoddy. He was a craftsman.

Let's dive more into this thought on craftsmen and workers in the Bible. Consider these thoughts from the *Holman Bible Dictionary*:

> The occupations and professions of ancient civilizations were, as in modern times, related to the natural resources, commerce, and institutions of the nations. Israel was no exception. Although readers of the Bible may be tempted to think of the Hebrews in general, and the Bible personalities in particular, as living lives totally absorbed by their religion, the ancients did have to make a living. In fact, few Hebrews followed a profession linked to the unique structure of their religion.
>
> In the course of time, occupations developed from simple tasks to more complex and from unskilled to skilled labor. This evolution was spurred by Israel's shift from a nomadic existence to a settled life and from a clan-type government to that of the monarchy. The development of secular occupations paralleled the settlement of the people into towns

and villages and the evolution of their government from a loose-knit tribal group to a nation involved in international politics. In earliest biblical times, the Hebrews followed their herds from pasture land to pasture land and water hole to water hole, though at times they lived for long periods near major cities. Their occupations were centered on the family enterprise.

When Israel entered into Canaan, the Hebrews moved toward a settled existence. As a settled people, agricultural pursuits became extremely important for survival. As the monarchy developed, many new occupations appear within the biblical text, mostly to maintain the royal house. Finally, as villages grew larger, and commerce between cities and nations expanded, various trades and crafts expanded with them. [emphasis added][2]

Commercial activity in the ancient Near East took many forms. The economy centered around agriculture, but some manufactured goods were produced and natural resources mined. Farm goods, products, and resources had to be transported to market centers and other countries. Barter and the buying and selling of goods and services held a prominent place in the life of villages and towns.

This is demonstrated by the large number of economic texts uncovered in excavations and the importance placed on transactional dialogue, and the use of commercial scenes to highlight major events in the biblical text. <u>Products, places of business, business practices (weights and measures, business law), and the means of transport all figure into the commercial picture of the biblical era.</u> [emphasis added][3]

The above commentary goes on to list 36 different jobs, roles, occupations, and titles in the Bible. All of us are inspired by the famous people or heroes of the Bible or by celebrity CEOs, notable workers, and other stories and personalities in the media that make the headlines. But here is what Helen Keller said: *"The world is moved along, not only by the mighty shoves of its heroes but also by the aggregate of the tiny pushes of each honest worker."*

I hope you can see that your work is indeed a ministry. You are not "just a carpenter" or "just a mechanic" or just a nurse, accountant, salesperson, or fill in the blank. No! Get rid of the word *just*. You are meant to do something useful and necessary that helps your fellow humans, helps the body of Christ, brings you joy, and glorifies God. It's biblical—it's HIS idea.

CHAPTER 3

CALLINGS, COMMANDS, AND JOURNEYS

N ow the LORD spoke to Moses, saying, 'See, I have called by name Bezalel, the son of Uri, the son of Hur, of the tribe of Judah. And I have filled him with the Spirit of God in wisdom, in understanding, in knowledge, and in all kinds of craftsmanship, to create artistic designs for work in gold, in silver, and in bronze, and in the cutting of stones for settings, and in the carving of wood, so that he may work in all kinds of craftsmanship. And behold, I Myself have appointed with him Oholiab, the son of Ahisamach, of the tribe of Dan; and in the hearts of all who are skillful I have put skill, so that they may make everything that I have commanded you'" (Exodus 31:1-6 NASB).

Your Work is a Gift and a Call

We all have experienced times and seasons in our lives when we took a job simply because we needed the money, particularly in our youth. I didn't like most of my teenage jobs. Sometimes you do what you've got to do. These can be times of learning and maturing. But given where you are now, do you know if you are called to do what you are currently doing? Is it fulfilling a desire of your heart? That can be a tough question, especially when you are younger.

I have seen people who simply knew what they wanted to do from the time they were young and set out on a course to do exactly that. I've always been a little envious of those people because I seemed to like everything. I pulled up some old notes in a scrapbook from when I was a little boy, and I wanted to be everything from an astronaut to a football player to a fireman. I still really didn't know what I wanted to do when I graduated high school. As I stated in chapter 1, it took me a while to realize and understand I had an ability and calling in sales and business. And that I had an ability in the specific industry in which I was working. I had a skill set that I didn't even recognize or appreciate.

That was perhaps my fault for always trying to chase something greener or more glamorous. Or at least more glamorous in my mind.

Years ago, while still working for the company selling video gear, I tried to go down the path of selling insurance and financial services. I was enamored with, or perhaps infatuated with, the idea of being a financial planner. I'd have a cool title, and I could wear a suit and tie to work (which I didn't mind at the time). I could potentially make good money. But it was not what I was good at. Although the subject matter interested me and I thought it was important, talking to people about estate planning and life insurance and selling financial products was actually not very enjoyable. I did not have enough *passion* for it. Could I have made a success of it? Yeah, maybe so, but I would have likely been frustrated and lacked true joy. And I would have missed God's BEST!

You need to be doing something you are passionate about. Passion will cause you to try harder and perfect your skills. It will also carry you through the tough times. If you know God called you to something or felt he has given you a particular talent and skill, then embrace it! (You will hear me repeat this phrase throughout this book.) You will reap far greater rewards and dividends. And if you know you were called, then when you encounter difficulties, you have an assurance that you are on the path God wants you to be on.

I'm always intrigued by people who have a seemingly "simple" job, yet they love it. Have you ever encountered somebody at an amusement park, a restaurant, a dry cleaner, or even at Walmart who has a smile on their face and greets you with a kind word? You can usually distinguish who enjoys their work and who doesn't. Or how about those in jobs that don't pay high salaries. An obvious example might be teachers or police officers. These people generally know they won't get rich in these professions, but they love their work. And thank God we have people in society who do love to work in these types of vocations. We need them to function in society. Imagine what life would be like if others weren't willing to serve in the vast myriad of positions that we depend on every day.

In the middle of writing this book, I was at a friend's house for a get-together. There was a man there I did not know, and after we were introduced, I asked what he did for a living. He said, "I serve the Lord through medical equipment sales." I loved that answer! I was so impressed with it; I'm trying to work it into my introduction to other people. But I thought it was such a succinct, clear statement: 1) I serve the Lord. 2) I do it with a skill and a job that he has given me. This guy had no idea I was writing this book, yet his answer to me seemed so timely. I'm going start using that, and so should you, "I serve the Lord through _____."

The Latin word *vocare* means "to call" and is the root of our modern word vocation. If you are unsure what your gift, skill, or calling is, I would recommend two things. First, ask yourself the following questions:

What is my desire?

What is my gift?

Where have I had favor?

When I was in my mid-twenties, I asked my pastor at the time, "How do I know what to do with my life or calling?" And this is what he asked of me: "desire, gift, favor." What is your heart's desire? What do you genuinely want to do? Where do you feel you have a gift? Where have others seen your gift? And where has God given you favor and opened doors? Dig deep into this for yourself. Do some careful analysis of your work, your relationships, and the things you gravitate toward. Be honest with yourself. I was a little late in life doing this. I had this desire to have my own business. The gifting was there, but I had to develop it. I also had to examine the areas of my life and work where I truly had favor and where my gift was acknowledged. Finally, as mentioned in chapter 1, it clicked with me one day on my job: "I'm pretty good at this. Why fight it?" As I said before, learn to embrace it, to embrace who you are.

I have a book on my shelf entitled *Why You Can't Be Anything You Want To Be* by Arthur Miller. Sort of an unusual title, and it may even seem not too positive at first glance. But in it, the author basically says we are hardwired as children, created and predisposed in a certain way. So why not work with it? Miller states, "You may function adequately at a job and even forge an impressive career. But unless you do what is lit by an inner fire, you're just getting by. Because the truth is, you were created with an indelible highly personal pattern of innate giftedness and motivation." He goes on to say, "The heart of a seven days a week faith lies in using one's endowed giftedness to serve the world with excellence and, through that service, to love and honor God" [emphasis added]. [4]

Your calling is also not just for you. It is for other purposes as well. Bezalel was called to help build the tabernacle under the supervision of Moses. That was his assignment. It was a necessary and worthy task, and he was gifted and skilled to accomplish it. He is mentioned three times in Exodus 31. (God also singles out Oholiab, who was appointed to help Bezalel.) I think God was actually quite proud of Bezalel and counted on him to get the job done.

This leads to the second thing I'd recommend. As a practical matter, I would also suggest taking a skills test, assessment test, or a personality profile if you haven't already. There is a list of these mentioned at the end of this book. There are many good ones out there. I have taken multiple tests over the years. So even if you've done this before, you should consider doing it again. You may find that although you have a core competency and skill, your desire and priorities and/or God's particular plans can change over the years. What I thought was important to me or what my desires were in my 20s I now find in my 50s are different in many ways. There are seasons of life when the specifics of your calling may be different. But please recognize you are a skilled craftsman for God and have unique abilities to share, no matter what those are or what stage of life you are in. As I heard Pastor Bill Scheer say, "Don't sleepwalk through life." Find out what you are good at and what you are meant to do.

Think about these familiar Scriptures, but look at them through the lens of your work and career:

"Do not neglect the gift that is in you" (1 Timothy 4:14 NKJV).

"Therefore do not be foolish, but understand what the Lord's will is" (Ephesians 5:17 NIV).

"I will give thanks to You, because I am awesomely and wonderfully made" (Psalm 139:14 NASB).

"'For I know the plans that I have for you,' declares the LORD, 'plans for prosperity and not for disaster, to give you a future and a hope'" (Jeremiah 29:11 NASB).

"God never changes his mind when he gives gifts or when he calls someone" (Romans 11:29 GW).

Sometimes, the very thing you may take for granted, or may not see in yourself, can be the catalyst that propels you into more meaningful work or to another level of success. Be who you are supposed to be, not who somebody else thinks you should be. (As I did when I tried to pursue a wrong career.) Don't misunderstand me: God will often ask us to take a step of faith or do something that seemingly is beyond ourselves. And there is certainly a place and time to stretch and grow, expand your capacity, and work on personal development. You may have to do things that are uncomfortable, but you must be true to who you are and live out your calling. Be the best version of you that you can possibly be.

Your Work is a Command

Notice in Exodus 31 at the beginning of this chapter that God called Bezalel and COMMANDED that he, Moses, and others build the tabernacle. Have you ever thought that not developing your skill or fulfilling your task is disobedience? It is violating God's command. By not following God's calling, you are disobeying his command. And God has some very strong thoughts about disobedience. Conversely, think of the rewards, joy, pleasure, and blessings of obeying. Look at these Scriptures:

"If you are willing and obedient, / You will eat the best of the land" (Isaiah 1:19 NASB).

"Have every skillful person among you come, and make all that the Lord has commanded" (Exodus 35:10 NASB).

"The Lord will open for you His good storehouse, the heavens, to give rain to your land in its season and to bless every work of your hand" (Deuteronomy 28:12 NASB).

Sometimes, the very thing you may take for granted, or may not see in yourself, can be the catalyst that propels you into more meaningful work or to another level of success.

Deuteronomy 28 is a chapter full of the warnings of disobedience and the rewards of obedience.

The commandment of Jesus to the disciples was clear and direct: "Follow Me." That implies that there is then a choice to be made. To follow or not follow. To heed the call or not heed the call. To obey or to disobey. Even though it cost them everything, think of what the disciples would have missed by not obeying.

In the recent video series entitled "The Chosen," which chronicles the life of the disciples, there is part of the story that seeks to explore and attempts to develop the character of Nicodemus and his interaction with Jesus. There is a scene where Jesus has encouraged Nicodemus to follow him and you see the struggle that Nicodemus is having as a prominent Jewish priest and rabbi. A short while later, the disciples are about to embark on a journey, and Nicodemus secretly leaves a bag of money for them but hides around the corner to see what happens. Jesus perceives what is going on, and you can see in his eyes and his heart that he wants Nicodemus to join them.

The next scene shows Nicodemus hiding around the corner, and he begins to weep. You see the struggle in his mind and in his heart about what to do. He knows the Messiah is there, but he just cannot make the hard choice. The camera pivots back to Jesus, and he sighs and says to Himself, "You came so close." I realize they may have taken some artistic license, but this sequence was very powerful to me. How many of us have come so close, but we just didn't quite do what God told us to do? How life might have been different? But God is rich in mercy and faithful and just to redeem us and forgive us. So, if you feel like you've missed it over the years, resolve to obey him today.

In Genesis 22:18, the Lord says to Abraham, "And in your seed all the nations of the earth shall be blessed, because you have <u>obeyed</u> My voice" (NASB, emphasis added). Could we perhaps apply this to our working lives and say, "Other businesses, people, employees, customers, and my church will be blessed because I obeyed the command of the Lord"? I think we can. Your obedience will influence and bless the lives of others. Being obedient to your call will open doors for you that might not have otherwise been opened.

Yes, it pays to obey!

Your Work is a Journey

Following your calling is also a journey. You read about my journey in the opening chapter. Your work may take you down several different paths throughout your life. For example, even though you may have studied engineering in college and that was what God told you to do, you may find yourself using that knowledge and skill in a different capacity at different points in life. Perhaps what starts as a career in structural engineering may become helping build churches on the mission field, providing relief in disasters, or simply sitting on your church's building committee. You just never know where simple obedience will take you.

Bezalel was not Moses, he was not Aaron, he was not Joshua, and he was not Caleb. But God placed in him a skill and a talent and appointed him for a specific task that was vital to God's plan. I'm

Being obedient to your call will open doors for you that might not have otherwise been opened.

not the CEO of a Fortune 500 company; I'm not a supervising engineer at a Boeing plant. I'm not a lawyer. These things are not what I do, nor what I'm gifted at. But like Bezalel, you and I still have a role to play in God's plan. I have simply been a faithful church member, lay person, and small business owner over the years. It has all been a part of my journey. Every step of my working life, every job I've had or interaction in the marketplace has been a growing and learning opportunity that prepared me for where I am now. Different seasons in life will require different things from you. But it's all part of the journey.

My friend Phil is a CPA. When he was a young man, he was working at Disney when he had a radical salvation experience. God told him to "spread the Word." As a result, he wanted to do great things for God and be in "ministry." He now thought the secular work wasn't worth the effort. He already had an MBA, but he so wanted to serve God he enrolled in Bible school part-time and got a degree in theology. Shortly after that, he took a job at a church in their finance department as an executive pastor. Just one problem—he didn't like it! In his words, "I was miserable." After two years, he left.

He sent out hundreds of resumes and barely got an interview. He was asking himself, "Lord, what is going on here?" Someone told him during this time, "You should hang out your own shingle." Phil now says, "That was probably prophetic, but I just didn't know it." Then a man reached out to Phil to ask for help with his

CPA practice. He had more work than he could handle and just did a fee split with Phil. This led to Phil developing his own client base and then working to help solve IRS tax problems. Today, now in his 60s, Phil and his wife have a thriving business, sit on various ministry boards and committees, pray for people in his office, and are tremendous financial supporters of the gospel. I recently asked Phil if he thought about retiring or exiting the business, and he said, "No, I'm having too much fun." I'm sure Phil would be the first to tell you there is no way he could have planned or predicted this journey. But wouldn't you agree that Phil is one of God's Craftsmen and is "in the ministry"?

Sometimes your calling finds you just like the accounting practice found Phil. And sometimes, the path you take may not be the path of least resistance. It may seem like a meandering road or that nothing is working as you had hoped or planned. But faith and faithfulness will get you to your destination. Proverbs 20:6 (NKJV) says, "Who can find a faithful man?" but Proverbs 28:20 (NKJV) goes on to say, "A faithful man will abound with blessings."

One of the best examples of this is the story of Joseph. You recall he had a dream as a young man that his brothers would bow before him. His brothers didn't like that story, so they betrayed him and sold him as a slave. He was sent to Egypt and had many setbacks, including imprisonment and false accusations. Yet, he remained faithful. I believe even he didn't realize his dream had come true until a pivotal moment when his brothers were standing in front of him. In one sense, he may have even forgotten about his dream by the time he was a leading figure in Egypt. Or perhaps the dream was not necessarily at the forefront of his mind.

Then one day, his brothers all showed up in his court, and they bowed to him, not even recognizing that it was Joseph (see Genesis 42:6-9). I suspect a flood of memories and emotions overwhelmed him. The Bible says he "turned away from them and wept" (Genesis 42:24 NASB). His calling had found him. The long arduous "journey" now made sense. I believe he suddenly realized, "All I've been through, all I've endured, all the setbacks, all the disappointments over the years—it was all meant for this moment." As I heard a minister say once, sometimes life and life's events, or our callings and special moments, are like a tapestry. On the one side, it's threads and strands, looking seemingly haphazard with no rhyme or reason. But on the other side, you see a beautiful pattern, carefully orchestrated weaves, creating a work of art woven together for a purpose.

In my own life, with the business success I've enjoyed, I would have never predicted or planned where I am today. I tried my best to make the right decisions each step of the way and do my best every day. Yet, despite my mistakes and sometimes lack of understanding, in hindsight, I can see each stop on the journey, all my daily work, my various jobs—all of it prepared me and laid a foundational stone to be where I am now.

We all have a call to do something, a command to obey God, and a journey to walk out. As my father-in-law said, "Find your place in the race, set a goal for your role, and keep your eyes on the prize."

CHAPTER 4

RUN YOUR RACE

Therefore, since we also have such a great cloud of witnesses surrounding us, let's rid ourselves of every obstacle and the sin which so easily entangles us, and let's run with endurance the race that is set before us, looking only at Jesus, the originator and perfecter of the faith (Hebrews 12:1, 2 NASB).

What would happen if you showed up to a track meet with a kayak and said, "I'm here for the race!" Or maybe you wanted to enter the Iditarod and came with only track shoes. Or worse, came with cats instead of sled dogs. What if you were a swimmer and tried running the 100-meter hurdles in your swimsuit and with bare feet? Or what if you were a basketball player, but tried to apply the same training, rules, and process to a baseball game?

These might be absurd examples, but I think you see the point. Hebrews 12:1 says to run the race "set before you." This Scripture is referring to our general, broad, overarching race as a Christian. But I think it also has meaning for our own individual race. The race we are individually called to run. The race at which we will have the most success, and the race that brings us satisfaction. And the race that we are to properly train for. It is also the race that we will be judged on.

"Tell Archippus, 'See to the ministry which you have received in the Lord, so that you may <u>fulfill it</u>.'" (Colossians 4:17 NASB, emphasis added).

"But you should keep a clear mind in every situation. Don't be afraid of suffering for the Lord. Work at telling others the Good News, and <u>fully carry out</u> the ministry God has given you" (2 Timothy 4:5 NLT, emphasis added).

Notice these verses talk about "FULFILLING" your call, your ministry, your RACE. That does not mean showing off or trying to best your fellow brothers and sisters in the Lord. That becomes an unhealthy pride or unhealthy competition. But do you really think God wants you in your race to lose? No, He wants you to win. And by win, I mean to <u>fulfill</u> what He wants you to accomplish and to receive your heavenly AND earthly rewards.

What race are you running? Too often I think we get caught up in the "rat race." We in America start chasing everything: new car, new TV, soccer games, a nice SUV, a bigger house, impressing the boss, climbing the ladder, etc. I've been there and done that too. These things, both literally and figuratively, are not necessarily wrong. But they can get us off track or preoccupied with things outside what we are supposed to be doing. They can hinder our ability to run our race. Sadly, many of us, and I think men in particular, wake up one day and say, "Am I climbing the right ladder?", "What 'race' am I running?", or "Why am I even in this particular race?"

Are you running the race set before you? Or put another way, are you running YOUR race? Are there weights or sin that are entangling you? These are hard but serious questions you should ask yourself. We should all periodically take inventory of our lives. But if you are feeling a particular dissatisfaction with your work, maybe some serious self-reflection or assessment is in order. I did this when I was making the attempt to work in financial services. I concluded that was the wrong race for me to run.

Other versions of Colossians 4:17 say to "take heed" or "pay attention." Perhaps you are out of balance. You could be in the right race, but you are taking on too many other things that are slowing you down. Or you may be in the wrong race, and in order to compensate for your dissatisfaction, you are getting entangled with tasks, material things, television, bad habits, etc. that are keeping you from moving into the right race to run.

Are you perhaps getting entangled?

Notice Hebrews 12:1 also says to "lay aside" the things that "entangle us." You would never want to run a sprint with an extra 50-pound sack on your back. Nor would you want to try to swim with bungee cords or ropes on your feet. Why? Because it slows you down. It makes the race that much harder. It drains your energy. And it limits your chance of success.

I'm not saying these things to be a downer, I'm saying them to help you be liberated. Could it be that work becomes a drudgery because we are working for the wrong reasons? Could it be that you feel trapped, entangled, or enslaved? Jesus said, "My yoke is easy and my burden is light." Listen to these words:

But do you really think God wants you in your race to lose? No, He wants you to win. And by win, I mean to fulfill what He wants you to accomplish.

"'Come to Me, all who are weary and burdened, and I will give you rest. Take My yoke upon you and learn from Me, for I am gentle and humble in heart, and you will find rest for your souls. For My yoke is comfortable, and My burden is light" (Matthew 11:28-30 NASB).

What does yoke mean? There is the physical yoke, usually associated with an animal or animals, such as a pair of oxen, that allows them to pull in unison. Webster's Dictionary says:

"A: a wooden bar or frame by which two draft animals (such as oxen) are joined at the heads or necks for working together

B: a frame fitted to a person's shoulders to carry a load in two equal portions

C: a clamp or similar piece that embraces two parts to hold or unite them in position"

The above is a practical, physical definition. Notice it refers to a "joining" together. But there is also a "spiritual yoke." Listen to this explanation from GotQuestions.org:

> A yoke is a wooden crosspiece fastened over the necks of two animals and attached to a plow or cart. A yoke allows two animals to share a load and pull together. Yokes were used in Bible times

primarily with bulls or oxen to plow fields and pull wagons. The animals yoked together needed to be close in size and weight for the cart or plow to pull evenly.

In the Bible the yoke is sometimes referenced metaphorically to describe the weight of a task or obligation. For example, King Rehoboam tried to instill respect for himself by threatening his subjects with "a heavy yoke" (1 Kings 12:11). Breaking a yoke often symbolized freedom from oppressors (Isaiah 10:27) or the beginning of a new phase in life, as when Elisha left his agrarian life to follow Elijah (1 Kings 19:19–21).

People in Jesus' day readily understood analogies using a yoke. They knew what Jesus meant when He said, "Come to me, all you who are weary and burdened, and I will give you rest. Take my yoke upon you and learn from me, for I am gentle and humble in heart, and you will find rest for your souls. For my yoke is easy and my burden is light" (Matthew 11:28–30). **An "easy" yoke meant that the burden being shouldered was not heavy because Jesus Christ would be pulling with us.**

Another place in Scripture uses the imagery of

a yoke to discourage Christians from entering into intimate dealings with unbelievers: "Do not be yoked together with unbelievers. For what do righteousness and wickedness have in common? Or what fellowship can light have with darkness? What harmony is there between Christ and Belial? Or what does a believer have in common with an unbeliever? What agreement is there between the temple of God and idols? For we are the temple of the living God" (2 Corinthians 6:14–16). To be "yoked together" is to be in a binding relationship. The warning in this passage is that a Christian should not enter a compromising personal or professional arrangement with a non-Christian. Two animals **unequally yoked** would end up fighting each other and the yoke. When the Israelites chased after idols, they were said to be yoking themselves to Baal (Psalm 106:28; Numbers 25:5). New Testament believers should be separated from the world … We should be careful whose yoke we accept and with whom we are yoked together. [emphasis added][5]

When we are "yoked" with Christ, it is true we are his servant. But serving him actually brings liberty. It brings us rest. Are you restless in your mind and spirit? Perhaps you are entangled. Maybe you are running the wrong race. Or maybe you are running the right race in a wrong way. When we take on his "yoke" and run our race for him, we become disentangled from the affairs of this world, we ease our burden, and we find rest for our souls. He will be pulling with the yoke. And we know He will be with us to help us win this race.

In 2 Timothy 4 (NASB), Paul knows he is at the end of his life. He's giving an admonition to Timothy and says in verse 7, "I have fought the good fight, I have finished the race, I have kept the faith." Some versions use the word "course" instead of race. I heard Myles Munroe preach on this once, and he said—and I'm paraphrasing—"Don't die old and feeble, die finished!!" Live your life and run your race so you know that when you have completed it, you're done and you're ready to go. I don't plan on dying for a long time, but that always stuck with me. "Die finished!" What a wonderful way to depart this earth, to be able to say, "I have run my race, I've completed my course."

A cautionary word is due here. We all know successful athletes train very regularly. We watch the results on television, but we never see the hours in the gym or on the field, or perhaps the diet restrictions or the study. There is self-discipline and there is a cost. Running your race will cost you something, and it may not always be easy. It could be time. It could be giving up other things in your life. It could require some financial sacrifices, at least temporarily. It may require you to reorient your life or change relationships. You may even go through some very difficult and trying circumstances. Hebrews 12:2 (NASB) says, "Looking only at Jesus, … who for the joy set before Him endured the cross." Learn to push through that time of enduring, so you can finish and fulfill your race.

At the beginning of this chapter, our subject verse was Hebrews 12:1, 2 where it references a "cloud of witnesses." The preceding chapter, Hebrews 11, is known as the "faith" chapter and mentions all the heroes

What a wonderful way to depart this earth, to be able to say, "I have run my race, I've completed my course."

of faith who went before us. It certainly takes faith to run your race. But read Hebrews 11 and see how many "races" were run by these men and women.

It starts with Abraham, who was not a prophet or a king. He was actually a merchant, a trader, a businessman, a craftsman in his own way. And he is referred to as the "father of our faith." It goes on to talk about great exploits, from people of all walks of life and all sorts of backgrounds.

> And what more shall I say? For time will fail me
> if I tell of Gideon, Barak, Samson, Jephthah,
> of David and Samuel and the prophets, who
> by faith conquered kingdoms, performed acts
> of righteousness, obtained promises, shut the
> mouths of lions, quenched the power of fire, escaped

the edge of the sword, from weakness were made strong, became mighty in war, put foreign armies to flight. (Hebrews 11:32-34 NASB)

Those who ran their race are watching us run our race! Jesus is also watching our race, cheering us on, and helping us carry his yoke. I think the Message Bible sums it up quite well:

Do you see what this means—all these pioneers who blazed the way, all these veterans cheering us on? It means we'd better get on with it. Strip down, start running—and never quit! No extra spiritual fat, no parasitic sins. Keep your eyes on *Jesus*, who both began and finished this race we're in. Study how he did it. Because he never lost sight of where he was headed—that exhilarating finish in and with God—he could put up with anything along the way: Cross, shame, whatever. And now he's *there*, in the place of honor, right alongside God. When you find yourselves flagging in your faith, go over that story again, item by item, that long litany of hostility he plowed through. *That* will shoot adrenaline into your souls! (Hebrews 12:1-3 MSG)

Are you ready to run YOUR race? ***On Your Mark... Get Set... GO!!***

CHAPTER 5

BECOMING A CRAFTSMAN

So now we know work is God's idea, that we have gifts and callings we must follow and be obedient to, and that we have a race to run. So how do we become a craftsman?

As the children of Israel were leaving Egypt, they came to Mount Sinai and Moses received the Ten Commandments from the Lord. Then they were instructed to build the tabernacle.

"Then Moses said to the sons of Israel, 'See, the LORD has called by name Bezalel the son of Uri, the son of Hur, of the tribe of Judah. And He has filled him with the Spirit of God, in wisdom, in understanding, in knowledge, and in all craftsmanship; to create designs for working in gold, in silver, and in bronze, and in the cutting of stones for settings and in the carving of wood, so as to perform in every inventive work. He also has put in his heart to teach, both he and Oholiab, the son of Ahisamach, of the tribe of Dan. He has filled them with skill to perform every work of an engraver, of a designer, and of an embroiderer, in violet, purple, *and* in scarlet *material*, and in fine linen, and of a weaver, as performers of every work and makers of designs" (Exodus 35:30-35 NASB).

There are several things to note in this passage, and the margin of my Bible mentions four: Bezalel was called by name; God filled him wisdom and understanding; God gave him skill—a talent, a gift, a willing heart.

1) Bezalel Was Called

We already talked about the gifts and callings of God. The point I want to emphasize here is how God singled him out for something specific. God "called by name Bezalel," and God also singles out Oholiab (called Aholiab in some translations) in Exodus 31:6, saying "I Myself have appointed with him Oholiab" (NASB). We see this over and over in Scripture: Abraham, Moses, Joshua, Gideon, David, the disciples, and Paul are all called by God. These are major figures, but how many times have minor or secondary figures of the Bible been called by God to help execute his plan?

Gideon had a monumental mission, but God chose 300 men to accompany him. We don't know them by name, but their roles and tasks were still significant.

A widow was called to feed Elijah and received a miracle.

Gehazi was called alongside Elisha.

Abishai was a right-hand man to David.

Paul gets much of the fame, but Silas and Barnabas were alongside him on many of his journeys. And in 2 Timothy 4:11 (NASB), he says, "Take along Mark and bring him with you, for he is useful to me for service."

Paul frequently closes his letters with references to friends, workers and laborers in ministry, elders of the church, and many more. ***Just because your name is not in the headlines, do not diminish the role you have to play in God's plan.***

2) Filled with Wisdom and Understanding

"And He has filled him with the Spirit of God, in wisdom, in understanding, in knowledge, and in all craftsmanship" (Exodus 36:31 NASB).

I define knowledge or understanding as more of a tactical thing, knowing what to do or how to do it. Wisdom is knowing whether or not I *should* do it, if it's the appropriate thing to do, or the right time. It's how you apply knowledge. For example, recently I knew it was time to hire another salesperson. Knowledge involves placing ads, where to place them, who to talk to, writing a job description, proper compensation, etc. Wisdom is getting the right fit for the team, getting the right person of character, and knowing when it is the right time to add to the staff.

Proverbs speaks over and over about getting wisdom and getting understanding. "Wisdom is the principal thing" say several versions of Proverbs 4:7. I have asked for and received God's wisdom in my work life over and over again. I depend on it! I study and train and try to do, know, and learn what I need to. Yet so often, situations arise where you simply are not sure what to do or how to respond. That is where the wisdom of God kicks in. Many times, it's just a creative idea or maybe an alternative that I hadn't previously thought of. Or sometimes it is dealing with the situation in a new way.

Just because your name is not in the headlines, do not diminish the role you have to play in God's plan.

Proverbs 2:10-12 (NLT) says, "For wisdom will enter your heart, and knowledge will fill you with joy. Wise choices will watch over you.

Understanding will keep you safe. Wisdom will save you from evil people."

James 1:5 in the Modern English Version says, "If any of you lacks wisdom, let him ask of God, who gives to all men liberally and without criticism, and it will be given to him."

God fills his craftsmen and craftswomen with wisdom and understanding that others do not have.

3) Skill and Talent

"He has filled them with skill to perform every work" (Exodus 35:35 NASB).

According to rabbinical tradition, when God determined to appoint Bezalel architect of the tabernacle, He asked Moses whether the choice was agreeable to him and received the reply: "Lord, if he is acceptable to Thee, surely he must be so to me!" I really believe that Bezalel and Oholiab were excellent craftsmen and the best people for the job. Even today, in Jerusalem there is a school named the Bezalel Academy of Arts and Design. According to Wikipedia, "The art created by Bezalel's students and professors in the early 1900s is considered the springboard for Israeli visual arts in the 20th century." [6]

Again, we've talked about this previously, but having skill, talent, and being excellent at what you do is crucial to success. You have to develop your skills and constantly work on improvement. Athletes such as Michael Jordan, Michael Phelps, Peyton Manning, Tiger Woods, and many others were certainly gifted and have achieved great success. But a behind the scenes look will reveal that they practiced, and practiced, and practiced. When they made a mistake, they learned from it. This applies to music, arts, business, woodworking, preaching, communication ... your job ... everything.

Have you ever heard of L. P. Ladouceur? He played for the Dallas Cowboys. His position was long snapper. He was the guy that hikes the ball to the punter and the field goal placeholder. You likely have not heard of him, but he made a 15-year career at this position. (And probably made a great living at it!) He had a seemingly undistinguished task, but a highly important job for the team. If he did not execute, the consequences could be disastrous. But he had developed his skill and become a craftsman at the long snapper position.

I know in my business, we've carved out and excelled in a sports niche of our industry. It has served us very well. Maybe there is a niche, skill, underserved market or unique service or product you could develop a skill in, either individually or corporately.

In this story of Bezalel, God goes on to talk about others who were working on building the tabernacle.

"And in the hearts of all who are skillful I have put skill, so that they may make everything that I have commanded you" (Exodus 31:6 NASB).

"'Have every skillful person among you come and make all that the LORD has commanded'" (Exodus 35:10 NASB).

In Exodus 35 through Exodus 36:7, the word "skill" or "skillful" is mentioned no less than nine times in the NASB version. In the NKJV version, the word is translated "gifted." Once you've identified your skill, talent, and gift, go all in and be the best you can be at it. Determine to excel in your lane or in your space, in your industry, and your sphere of influence.

4) A Willing Heart

"'Take from among you a contribution to the LORD; whoever is of a willing heart is to bring it as the LORD's contribution'" (Exodus 35:5 NASB).

"'He also has put in his heart to teach'" (Exodus 35:34 NASB).

In that same passage of Exodus 35 through 36:7 mentioned above, there are six instances where the phrase "a willing heart" or a reference to the people's "heart" is used. If you are going to let God use you as a craftsman, you first must have an open and willing heart—you must be open to how He has created you and to what He is asking YOU to do. And do it with the proper attitude.

"Then Moses called Bezalel and Aholiab, and every gifted artisan in whose heart the LORD had put wisdom, **everyone whose heart was stirred, to come and do the work**" (Exodus 36:2 NKJV, emphasis added).

The heart is where the mind and spirit merge. Sometimes your spirit wants to do something, but your mind seems to fight it. But when spirit and mind agree, then there is clarity and power and things seem to get much easier.

Remember Isaiah 1:19 says, "If you are **willing** and obedient, you will eat the best of the land" (NASB, emphasis added). The "willing" is where your heart lies. And it can be as simple as your attitude or how you view things. Most parents can probably relate to this, but my wife used to tell the kids when they were small to go pick up their room. They would stomp up the stairs and begrudgingly do it. Although they obeyed, their attitude was poor, and their heart was not in it.

We attend a church that has two Sunday services, with hundreds of people in each service. Week after week, I see virtually the same people guiding cars in the parking lot, smiling and greeting at the door, serving coffee, checking in children. Almost always with a smile on their face. Routine stuff, normal tasks, nothing super complicated … what's the difference? Might it be that a willing heart to serve is in these volunteers? Have you examined your heart?

If you want to increase your ability to be an effective craftsman, think about having a willing heart and increasing your service both in a practical sense, such as volunteering for your church, but also in a business sense. How can you better serve those you interact with every day: your co-workers, employees, customers? Even Jesus said he came not to be served, but to serve. His heart was willing.

Just a side thought … don't forget to show appreciation to those who serve you. After walking by the same traffic coordinator at church for weeks, I finally asked him his name. I told him how I appreciated him serving us this way. I received a warm "Thank you," and a smile was on his face.

Putting it All Together

One of the best examples I can think of on becoming a craftsman is my wife, Brenda. Years ago, we took a trip to visit some friends and she saw a fake decorative pie at a store. She liked it and was tempted to buy it, but then thought, "I think I could make this at home and save a little money." She was a stay-at-home mom at the time, so when we returned from our trip, she went to the store, grabbed a book on dough art, and began experimenting while the kids were at school. I came home from work one day, and lo and behold, she had made a fake pie.

She has always been a good cook and has a gift with food and does have an artistic side to her as well. All of this seemed to come together in the form of creating decorative fake foods and drinks. After making that first fake pie, she began to make other things and then thought, "I wonder if people would buy these?" We happened to be coming up on our neighborhood garage sale, which was very big in our community. She set out all her creations and in four to five hours on a Saturday morning sold $400 worth of goods. Now she's on to something! I'm proud to say 25 years later she is still going strong.

I believe she was "called by name" to do this; that God has given her wisdom and skill, which she has continually developed; and that she has a willing heart to obey and keep at it. This gift and talent of hers allowed her to be a stay-at-home mom with a flexible schedule, provide additional income to our household, and flourish while working at something she loves to do. She now employs several women who also have mothering responsibilities, so she is able to accommodate. She has been on numerous radio and TV shows and even appeared on the Rachael Ray show. Her products have been featured in movies, like *The Muppets*, and many other places, such as the Walmart Museum in Bentonville. It all started with an idea and a desire, and then continuing and flowing and developing her gift. She will be the first to tell you it was a God-inspired idea. She became a craftsman ... actually, a CRAFTSWOMAN!

CHAPTER 6

STEWARDSHIP: WHAT'S IN YOUR HAND?

O nce you know what you are supposed to do with your vocation or career, and are working at becoming a craftsman or craftswoman, now what? One basic principle of the Bible is that we are stewards of all God has given us. Webster's Dictionary defines stewardship as "the careful and responsible management of something entrusted to one's care." You are to be a steward of the calling and gifts God has given you.

Most of us have heard the parable of the talents in the Bible. It reads as follows:

"For the kingdom of heaven is like a man traveling to a far country, who called his own servants and delivered his goods to them. And to one he gave five talents, to another two, and to another one, to each according to his own ability; and immediately he went on a journey. Then he who had received the five talents went and traded with them, and made another five talents. And likewise he who had received two gained two more also. But he who had received one went and dug in the ground, and hid his lord's money. After a long time the lord of those servants came and settled accounts with them.

"So he who had received five talents came and brought five other talents, saying, 'Lord, you delivered to me five talents; look, I have gained five more talents besides them.' His lord said to him, 'Well done, good and faithful servant; you were faithful over a few things, I will make you ruler over many things. Enter into the joy of your lord.' He also who had received two talents came and said, 'Lord, you delivered to me two talents; look, I have gained two more talents besides them.' His lord said to him, 'Well done, good and faithful servant; you have been faithful over a few things, I will make you ruler over many things. Enter into the joy of your lord.'

"Then he who had received the one talent came and said, 'Lord, I knew you to be a hard man, reaping where you have not sown, and gathering where you have not scattered seed. And I was afraid, and went and hid your talent in the ground. Look, there you have what is yours.'

"But his lord answered and said to him, 'You wicked and lazy servant, you knew that I reap where I have not sown, and gather where I have not scattered seed. So you ought to have deposited my money with the bankers, and at my coming I would have received back my own with interest. So take the talent from him, and give it to him who has ten talents.

'For to everyone who has, more will be given, and he will have abundance; but from him who does not have, even what he has will be taken away. And cast the unprofitable servant into the outer darkness. There will be weeping and gnashing of teeth.'" (Matthew 25:14-30 NKJV)

A careful study of this passage reveals that the master obviously expected a return on his investment, or a multiplication of the talents. The stewards were expected to give an account upon the master's return from his journey. Notice also that each one was given talents according to his ability. Three different levels of ability, yet they were not expected to stay at the level they began at. They were expected to grow and multiply their talents. So, it doesn't matter where you are currently—one, two, or five. You must ask yourself, "Am I giving my best effort to multiply my skill, my craft, my effectiveness? Am I becoming a better craftsman?"

Notice also that twice, the master said, "Well done, good and faithful servant," and each person was rewarded with more. It does not matter the starting point—God

You are to be a steward of the calling and gifts God has given you.

wants you to increase your talent, money, influence, and ability. At whatever level you currently are, He is pleased and rewards us when we multiply. The steward who hid his one talent never grew, never multiplied, never increased. He was in fear. In fact, he was called unprofitable and "wicked and lazy." He was severely reprimanded and thrown into darkness.

People sometimes get jealous of those who seemingly have a lot or have been blessed, and they ask themselves, "Why not me?" Well, maybe those blessed people were good and faithful stewards of what they were given. The Bible clearly states that those who are faithful and multiply will be given more (see verse 29).

Have you heard of the story "Acres of Diamonds"? In it, a man who is seeking riches and wealth embarks on a fruitless journey in pursuit of diamonds, never realizing he was sitting on the true riches and wealth the entire time. It reads as follows:

> Dr. Russell Conwell once went on a trip along the Tigris River in present-day Iraq, using a guide hired in Baghdad who would take him out to the Persian Gulf. These river guides were like barbers in that they liked to talk, but the story this one told, Conwell insists, is easily verified.
>
> There was a man, Al Hafed, who lived on the banks of the River Indus who had a nice farm with orchards and gardens, excess cash, a beautiful wife, and children. He was wealthy because he was contented. Then an old priest visited him and one night related how the world was made, including the formation of all the rocks, the earth, the precious metals, and stones. He told the farmer that if he had a few diamonds, he could have not just one farm but many. The farmer listened. Suddenly, he wasn't that happy with what he had thus far acquired in life.
>
> He sold up and went traveling in search of diamonds across Persia, Palestine, and into Europe. A couple

of years later, what money he had was gone, and he was wandering around in rags. When a large wave came in from the sea, he was happily swept under by it.

The man who had bought the farmer's land was another story. One day, watering his animals in the stream that ran through the property, he noticed a glint in the watery sands. It was a diamond. In fact, it was one of the richest diamond finds in history; the mines of Golconda would yield not just one or two but acres of diamonds.

Open your mind

In this tiny book, which is actually a transcript of a hugely popular lecture that he gave, Conwell relates similar true-life stories about the folly of going off to find your fortune when it is in your own backyard or just staring you in the face. He suggests that most people are 'pygmies of their possible selves because they are not willing to accept, or it did not occur to them, that they have great untouched powers: "Families do not credit their own folks with abilities they attribute to other persons. Towns and cities are cursed because their own people talk them down", he says.

Conwell's message is that <u>we shouldn't fall for the</u> <u>trap of thinking that all the great people and the great</u> <u>businesses are somewhere else.</u> Consider that Henry Ford started designing and building his car on his own farm and built the famous Ford production line factories in the same area where he had grown up. There was nothing special about Dearborn, Michigan - he made it special without ever leaving his own backyard. Warren Buffett, the great investor, decided against moving his family to Wall Street. He stayed in Omaha, Nebraska, and made his billions there. [emphasis added][7]

Have not all of us been guilty of this at one time or another in our lives? Pursuing and chasing something where we perceive the grass is greener? Or our attention gets focused on the shiny gold object off to the right or left instead of what's in front of us? For example, I previously spoke of my desire to be my own boss and have my own company. To do that, I tried to experiment with, perhaps even chase, several different things. I had moderate success, but nothing seemed to quite fit. But while working for the company selling video equipment, I was dissatisfied for some reason. Perhaps it was the environment, or maybe it was just my restlessness. I was probably also envious of other people who were having success in their business or endeavors. So I continued pursuing other things even though I was having success at what I was doing. It seems sometimes that we are so worried about who we are not, or what we cannot do, that we overlook or ignore who we are and what we can do. We fail to celebrate, embrace, and accept our role. I was guilty of this, but thankfully, I changed my thinking.

As I said earlier, after trying several different ideas, I suddenly realized, "Hey, I'm good at this. Maybe I should just leverage it for all I can and develop it as much as I can." So, in January of 2011, I started my own company. Long story short, I've never looked back. I've never regretted it. And I've had tremendous success. I have worked very hard, to be sure, and there have been a few sleepless nights. But I have been more satisfied, I've had more opportunities, and I've had more means to bless people than I thought I ever would. And I feel like I still have a lot of room to grow. While I've certainly made mistakes, I attribute a good portion of my success to finally realizing I had my own "Acres of Diamonds" and to also being a good steward of what God has given me. First, He gave me a talent, both literally and monetarily. Then I worked to steward it and multiply it. After all, it is his business, not mine. I'm just the steward.

> **It seems sometimes that we are so worried about who we are not, or what we cannot do, that we overlook or ignore who we are and what we can do. We fail to celebrate, embrace, and accept our role.**

So, where do you begin? Start with what's in your hand. Here's what Ben Cerullo says in an online article for Inspiration.org:

> I meet a lot of believers who feel like they simply don't have what it takes. They say they would do great things for God if they just had more money ... more time ... more energy ... or more people to help them.
>
> The mistake such people make is that they're focusing on what they *don't* have when the Lord wants them to realize what they *do* have. By simply shifting our focus, we can trade in our frustration and receive a life filled with miracles and abundance instead.
>
> Look at God's incredible question to Moses in Exodus 4:2:
>
> *"What is that in your hand?"*
>
> When the Lord asked this question, the only thing in Moses' hand was a crude shepherd's rod. It wasn't much. Just a piece of wood. An inanimate object. A tool of Moses' trade.

God was commissioning him for the daunting task of delivering over a million Israelites from slavery in Egypt. And all Moses had in his hand was the wooden staff he had used for 40 years to tend his flocks of sheep.

Do you see how powerful this message is for you and me? Like Moses, we're being called to do great things ... supernatural things ... things much bigger than we could ever accomplish without divine assistance.

Yet too often, we think our problem is that we lack some important ingredient or resource needed for success. "If only I had this or that ..." we complain.

But notice that God wasn't asking Moses to give Him something he didn't already have. Instead, He asked Moses, as He is asking us today ... "What's that in your hand?"

Moses had been carrying around that ordinary piece of wood for many years, and nothing dramatic had happened as a result. But after Moses surrendered the wooden rod to the Lord, it amazingly became *"the rod of God"* instead of merely the rod of Moses (Exodus 4:20). No longer a mere piece of wood, this rod enabled Moses to part the Red Sea, bring water out of a rock, and defeat enemy armies.

What is in *your* hand, my friend? Money? Time? Possessions? Influence? Some kind of special God-given aptitude?

If you're honest, the thing in your hand probably seems inadequate to meet the needs around you. However, you'll be amazed by what can happen when you surrender it to the Lord.[8]

I don't think I could say it any better than Ben Cerullo. Start with what is in your hand, develop your acres of diamonds, and be a faithful steward. Multiply what you have for God so you can hear those words, "Well done!"

CHAPTER 7

INCREASE AND CAPACITY

"May the LORD give you increase more and more,
You and your children.
May you be blessed by the LORD,
Who made heaven and earth" (Psalm 115:14-15 NKJV).

I have to give credit for this chapter to Dr. Bob Harrison, a friend, a mentor, a teacher, and the person from whom I learned the message of Increase. Learning this principle and teaching profoundly changed my thinking and my life as well as my outlook on business. What does this word increase really mean?

Webster says:

*"To make (something) larger or greater in size, amount, number, etc. **increase**. noun. English Language Learners Definition of **increase**: the act of becoming larger or of making something larger or greater in size, amount, number*

*To **increase** means to make greater, as in quantity, extent, or degree: Some synonyms might be addition, build up, expand, inflate, boost..."*

There is a principle that says anything not growing is either stagnant or decaying. So your life, your Christian walk, everything about you should be increasing. Anything you set your hand or mind to, anything important in your life should be increasing. We are talking about spirit, soul, and body. You should be improving your health, your mind, your learning, your income, your knowledge and capacity, and your effectiveness. And yes, increasing what you can do for the kingdom of God.

You should have an expectancy, an attitude, and a mind-set that there is more for you, more that God wants for you, and more that God wants <u>from</u> you. Why? So that you can reach your full potential and fulfill your calling and destiny. So you can be a better craftsman. And so you can bless others. I'm not necessarily saying that you will be a billionaire or have a church of 10,000 people or win a Super Bowl. I am just simply saying there is always another level you can reach in whatever you do or wherever you are in life. It starts with a mind-set that 1) God is good, 2) He wants this for you, and 3) you can actually achieve it! Are you willing to go for it? Are you willing to increase your capacity?

There is a saying I once heard that goes, "A mind once stretched can never return to its original dimensions." Once you understand and begin to live out this principle, it's hard to go back. You are now responsible for what you know and have learned. Jesus said, "No one, after putting his hand to the plow and looking back, is fit for the kingdom of God" (Luke 9:62 NASB). Are you willing to pay the price? There is a cost and a sacrifice to Increase and to being God's craftsman. Once you begin this journey, it can be a little intimidating at times, but the rewards are worth it.

As I wrote in the opening chapter, I had a very modest and perhaps disadvantaged background. Where I started in life was pretty small and limited by most measurements. Yet I have experienced a tremendous increase in my life. I have a wonderful wife, wonderful kids, health, a good income, and friends. My financial giving is more than it has ever been. Most importantly, I have the saving knowledge of Jesus Christ. I am blessed! I have increased! And I know if it can happen to me, for me, and IN me, it can happen to you too!

Increase, prosperity, and the blessings of God are not just about you and me. It's about what God wants us to do for others.

Desiring increase or desiring more from life is not wrong or evil. What could God's people do with more resources and finances? Think about the impact and difference we could make in this world if we would truly catch the desire of God's heart, which is to bless us to fulfill the mission he has for us. As God's craftsman, what could you do with an increase in your life? What kind of inheritance, both monetarily and otherwise, could you leave for your children or children's children? (See Proverbs 13:22.) How could you bless those less fortunate than you?

Remember the story of the good Samaritan? Remember he paid the bills of the injured man? He helped the man physically, took him to the inn, and then said, "Put it on my tab." I think it was Phil Pringle I heard once say, "Being a Christian is expensive." It takes money, time, and effort to feed the hungry, clothe the poor, and fund the gospel. It sometimes takes many resources to be an effective laborer and an effective craftsman for the kingdom. When we increase, we can become part of those resources and maybe an answer to someone else's prayer.

Just yesterday, in the middle of writing this book, at a men's lunch, I heard the pastor giving advice to a young man who said he was a small-business man but had some ideas for ministry that he wanted to do. The first thing this pastor said to him, and I'm paraphrasing a little, was, "Quit thinking of your business as a 'small' business. It's a BUSINESS. Make it big enough to do what you desire to do. Do you want to reach more people in this ministry capacity you're dreaming about? Then make your business big."

Remember the book *The Prayer of Jabez*? It is based on 1 Chronicles 4:10 (NLT), which says, "He was the one who prayed to the God of Israel, 'Oh, that you would bless me and expand my territory! Please be with me in all that I do, and keep me from all trouble and pain!' And God granted him his request." This is a simple prayer for increase. And God answered it.

In Genesis 13:2 (NASB), it says, "Abram was very rich in livestock, silver, and gold." Deuteronomy 1:11 (NASB) says, "May the LORD, the God of your fathers increase you a thousand times more than you are, and bless you, just as He has promised you!"

It sometimes takes many resources to be an effective laborer and an effective Craftsman for the kingdom. When we increase, we can become part of those resources and maybe an answer to someone else's prayer.

Look what happened in the story of Bezalel and the craftsmen. God called the people to build a tabernacle, and they brought offerings and materials, invested time and labor, and accomplished a great task. Remember ... it was a command of the Lord. Check this out:

"Then Moses called Bezalel, Oholiab, and every skillful person in whom the LORD had put skill, everyone whose heart stirred him, to come to the work to perform it. They received from Moses every contribution which the sons of Israel had brought to perform the work in the construction of the sanctuary. **And they still continued bringing to him voluntary offerings every morning. And all the skillful people who were performing all the work of the sanctuary came, each from the work which they were performing**, and they said to Moses, 'The **people are bringing much more than enough** for the construction work which the LORD commanded us to perform.' So Moses issued a command, and circulated a proclamation throughout the camp, saying, 'No man or woman is to perform work any longer for the contributions of the sanctuary.' **So the people were restrained from bringing any more. For the material they had was sufficient and more than enough for all the work, to perform it**" (Exodus 36:2-7 NASB, emphasis added).

Isn't that amazing!? Verses 6 and 7 say the people were restrained from bringing more because they had TOO MUCH. That is INCREASE! Part of being God's craftsman is flowing in his blessing so that you can have more than enough to benefit others. First Corinthians 15:58 (TPT) says, "So now, beloved ones, stand firm, stable, and enduring. Live your lives with an unshakable confidence. We know that we prosper and excel in every season by serving the Lord, because we are assured that our union with the Lord makes our labor productive with fruit that endures."

Let's view our daily work as a means to give out and find who we can bless and produce fruit that endures.

May I submit to you that if you think you should be a craftsman for God in a small way, you may need to think again? Increase your mind and your vision. You need to increase your capacity to

God does not do things halfway; God Increases! As a craftsman, you should always be increasing.

receive and your capacity to give out. Pray for new ideas. Expand your thinking. Wouldn't it be wonderful if you could say in your life or business or ministry that "the material was sufficient and more than enough"? Referring back to our story of the talents, what did the first two stewards do? They DOUBLED! Did God scold them? Was the master displeased? NO! He praised them and gave them more!

It's obvious from Scripture that the tabernacle Bezalel was building was not a rickety shack. No, it was an opulent and magnificent structure. God does not do things halfway; God increases! As a craftsman, you should always be increasing.

CHAPTER 8

THE SECRET WEAPON

hat if I told you I had a secret weapon to make you more successful in your endeavors? I bet you I could charge a lot of money for a seminar on this. Well, to me, it's quite simple but so often overlooked. And it's really not a secret. What I am referring to is the power and presence of the Holy Spirit.

If you are a born-again Christian, you know that God is a triune being: God the Father, God the Son, and God the Holy Spirit. We always sing and offer praise to God and Jesus, yet I think often we unwittingly ignore the Holy Spirit. He seemingly takes third place. I do not believe it is intentional. I think it's just something, or he is something, that's a little hard for our minds to grasp.

Although he has existed forever and appears in the Old Testament, the indwelling and baptism of the Holy Spirit is a New Testament dispensation. Remember that in Genesis, God said, "Let *US* make man in our image." Notice the plurality of that statement? It's the Father, the Son, and the Holy Spirit. When Jesus was baptized, you have the Son in the water, you have the voice from Heaven coming from God approving his Son, and the Spirit descending like a dove. All three were present at that moment.

I recently reread John Bevere's book *The Holy Spirit,* which I highly recommend. Although I have been a spirit-filled believer for my entire adult life, this was a breath of fresh air. I had to repent for ignoring the Holy Spirit. I feel I have a renewed understanding of his presence, his power, and his willingness to be my companion.

And I found I have a ready and willing business partner!

Jesus said, "It is to your advantage that I go away … [and] send Him to you" (John 16:7 NKJV). How often have we glossed over that statement? We all know the Spirit was continually active in the lives of the apostles in the book of Acts. Is he active in your life today? Particularly Monday through Friday? He is not meant to be relegated to a Sunday morning service! No, he is with us constantly, ready to commune, to help, to comfort, to guide. He is referred to as all these things, with all these adjectives. I believe it's the Holy Spirit who even prompted me to write this book. And as I seek him earnestly and have tried to dive deeper into my relationship with the Holy Spirit, I find ideas and thoughts and peace coming to me in a stronger way than they ever have. In 2020, we lived through the COVID-19 outbreak. I know for a certainty that it was the presence of the Holy Spirit that helped me through this time, both personally <u>and in my business.</u>

Have you ever invited the Holy Spirit into your office, into your cubicle, on the job site, or into your entire business? If you are a business owner, ask him to help you with your employees, your coworkers, your management, your marketing plans, and so on. Have you sought him for guidance and ideas on career moves or on how to solve a problem? It's quite simple: he is there ready and willing to help! I have so come to appreciate the Holy Spirit as part of the Godhead and what his presence means in my life and in my business! And I feel like I am just getting started.

In another book of John Bevere's, *X: Multiply Your God-Given Potential,* he refers to an extremely successful businessman who attributes his success to listening to the

And I found I have a ready and willing business partner!

voice of God and the Holy Spirit. He determined he would "walk with God" in the marketplace and listen to the Holy Spirit's voice, no different than a minister on the platform. He would listen to God's voice in quiet times as well as in business meetings. He has been led to tremendous deals and opportunities and financial rewards as a result of tapping into the mind of the Holy Spirit.

As Proverbs 3:5 says, "Trust in the Lord with all your heart [mind, spirit], and lean NOT on your own understanding" (NKJV, emphasis added). We must learn to LEAN on the voice and promptings of the Holy Spirit. He will give you creative ideas that you would never have come up with on your own. I remember Dr. David Yonggi Cho, pastor of the largest church in the world in Seoul, being asked once to what he attributed his church growth. He simply said, "I pray, and I obey." He was listening to the Holy Spirit.

I regularly attend Bob Harrison's Increase events, and one speaker I heard who owned a very large automotive parts distributor made this statement: "Being a Christian and having the Holy Spirit is a competitive advantage." How much better would your business be, your job performance be, or your joy and fulfillment increase by listening more closely to the Holy Spirit? Remember, God generally speaks in a still, small voice. I can tell you of numerous times when I was prompted to call a person, reach out to a client, purchase or not purchase certain inventory, had favor and introductions, or "just happened" to run across a deal … I have made several real estate investments that have turned out quite well ... I attribute all this success to listening to the Holy Spirit.

There is a little-known booklet or collection of writings called "The Columbus Prophecies." (Thank you, Phil H.) It documents the writings and inspirations of Christopher Columbus in his effort to sail to the West Indies. The following is an excerpt according to BYU Religious Studies Center:

How much better would your business be, your job performance be, or your joy and fulfillment increase by listening more closely to the Holy Spirit?

Historians have written about Columbus' first voyage to America from many points of view. Most secular historians, however, have placed little emphasis on the most important theme of all—the fact that Columbus was guided by the Spirit of God. Beginning with the decision Christopher made concerning his point of departure and continuing all the way through to his return voyage to Spain, and we can find numerous junctures at which the Lord manifested His hand in Columbus' key decisions.

Before 1492, other navigators had tried unsuccessfully to explore westward from the Azores Islands (800 miles west of the coast of Portugal), assuming that this was the best place from which to set sail (Morison 1:97–98). Although the Azores were the western-most islands known in the Atlantic, Columbus chose to sail from Palos, Spain, to the Canary Islands (off the west coast of Africa) and from there, to launch his voyage into the vast unknown. By doing so, he caught the trade winds blowing from the northeast to the southwest and avoided the headwinds which blow from the west to the east in the vicinity of the Azores (Nunn 37–38,42).

The route Columbus chose has stood the test of time: five hundred years of sailing have proven it the best possible course for sailing west from southern Europe to North America. Nunn suggested that Columbus' successful navigation was the result of "an application of reason to . . . knowledge" (Nunn 50). Columbus, however, gave credit to the Lord. Even though he was a successful seaman and an accomplished navigator, he said, "**With a hand that could be felt, the Lord opened my mind to the fact that it would be possible to sail from here to the Indies... This was a fire that burned within**

me; who can doubt that this fire was not merely mine, but also of the Holy Spirit. (West and Kling 105). [emphasis added][9]

Notice that Columbus was a skilled navigator and seaman—I think we can say he was a "craftsman." He applied reason and knowledge ... yet he himself attributed the planning and success of the voyage to the HOLY SPIRIT. Imagine that ... America was discovered because someone listened to the Holy Spirit!

John 16:13 (NASB) says, "'But when He, the Spirit of truth, comes, He will guide you into all the truth; for He will not speak on His own, but whatever He hears, He will speak; and He will disclose to you what is to come.'"

I call this a secret weapon because most people will never tap into the power of the Holy Spirit. But it's not a secret. He is available to anyone who will invite him into their job, work, or business. The ideas, the protection, the peace, and the power you will receive by partnering with the Holy Spirit will take you to places that you never thought you could go. Develop your relationship with him. And get ready for a wonderful ride and to soar to new heights!

CONCLUSION

You and I live in the most prosperous time in human history. Despite what may seem like trying times, I believe we are truly blessed to be alive now. We have many opportunities to choose what we do for a living that never existed before. I also believe God did not create us so we would live a dismal life, especially here in the 21st century.

So, what do we do now? As we've already laid out, I believe that being God's craftsman is for three primary and simple purposes:

- For Yourself

- For Others

- For God

For Yourself

When I say being God's craftsman is for yourself, that is not a selfish statement. If you are a Christian and a follower of Jesus, God wants you to have a blessed life. You are his child. Jesus said it is his Father's good pleasure to give you the kingdom of heaven. He created the garden for Adam. God's love is demonstrated throughout life and the Bible. Even when things don't go as planned or we don't understand the circumstances, God is still a good God. He is our heavenly father. His promises are "Yes and Amen." Deuteronomy 28 is full of promises and blessings if we are obedient. And He wants your life to be pleasurable and enjoyable, particularly in our daily walk and our daily work. I firmly believe this.

Proverbs 16:3 (NASB) says, "Commit your works to the LORD and your plans will be established."

And one of my favorite Scriptures is Psalm 37:4 (NASB), "Delight yourself in the LORD and He will give you the desires of your heart."

How about Jeremiah 29:11 (NASB): "'For I know the plans that I have for you,' declares the LORD, 'plans for prosperity and not for disaster, to give you a future and a hope.'"

You've probably read James 1:17 (NIV), "Every good and perfect gift is from above." I like how the Message Bible says it:

> "So, my very dear friends, don't get thrown off course. Every desirable and beneficial gift comes out of heaven. The gifts are rivers of light cascading down from the Father of Light. There is nothing deceitful in God, nothing two-faced, nothing fickle. He brought us to life using the true Word, showing us off as the crown of all his creatures" (v 16-18).

Remember the movie *Chariots of Fire?* In it, Eric Liddell says, "I believe *God made me* for a purpose, but He also made me *fast*. **And when I run, I feel His pleasure**" (emphasis added).

Do you feel his pleasure in your work? If not, pray how you might make that change. He wants you to enjoy your work as his craftsman. God is for you, and he wants you to succeed!

For Others

We have already laid this out in previous chapters, but if your only motivation is for your own selfish ambitions or strictly for monetary gain, then you missed the point. You are part of the human race, and part of the body of Christ. First Corinthians 12 talks about how every member, every organ, every limb, is part of the body and is crucial to the entire body functioning. We all need each other. In Russell Conwell's story about "Acres of Diamonds," he concludes by saying this:

"Greatness consists in doing great deeds with little means - in the accomplishment of vast purposes. It consists in the private ranks of life - in helping one's fellows, benefiting one's neighborhood, in blessing one's own city and state."

For God

We mentioned this Scripture in the beginning:

"'Your light must shine before people in such a way that they may see your good works and glorify your Father who is in heaven'" (Matthew 5:16 NASB).

Psalm 127:1 (NASB) says, "Unless the Lord builds a house, they who build it labor in vain."

If you fail to include God in your plans and fail to give him glory, whatever you are building will be in vain. What the Lord builds is fruitful labor and will stand. It's always my prayer that my heart posture is right and that I truly give God glory for all my success. I know I work very hard, and God expects us not to be lazy. But at the end of the day, he gets the glory. I know it was not my own strength or my own intellect that got me this far, and it certainly is not what will take me to where I still need to go.

Psalms 115:1 (NKJV) says, "Not unto us, O LORD, not unto us, but to Your name give glory." The Contemporary English Version says, "We don't deserve praise! The LORD alone deserves all of the praise."

Amen to that!

I could write even more about faith, prayer, God's favor, honor, integrity, creativity, and so on. These are all vital and important topics and areas of life in which to follow God. I trust that you understand these Christian teachings and principles are essential to being God's craftsman. I chose the topics and subjects of emphasis to include in this book because I think they are key points of power and key areas to develop for all of us who work in the marketplace and interact with the secular world.

Remember our friend Bezalel? Let's take another look at our key passage.

"Now the LORD spoke to Moses, saying, 'See, I have called by name Bezalel, the son of Uri, the son of Hur, of the tribe of Judah. And I have filled him with the Spirit of God in wisdom, in understanding, in knowledge, and in all kinds of craftsmanship, to create artistic designs for work in gold, in silver, and in bronze, and in the cutting of stones for settings, and in the carving of wood, so that he may work in all kinds of craftsmanship. And behold, I Myself have appointed with him Oholiab, the son of Ahisamach, of the tribe of Dan; and in the hearts of all who are skillful I have put skill, so that they may make everything that I have commanded you'" (Exodus 31:1-6 NASB).

I encourage you to take these verses and this story personally. I'd like for you to recite the verses and insert your name and your vocation as best as you can and make it a personal confession. It might go something like this:

God has called me (your name) a son/daughter of the Lord, a child of God, and God has filled me with the spirit of wisdom, understanding, and knowledge in all kinds of skill and craftsmanship that I might build, sell, create (your profession, your vocation or job description) and be a light in the marketplace. And God has appointed others to help me and has given me favor, and God has put in their hearts to use their skills to help me so that I might accomplish everything that God has commanded me to do.

Ephesians 2:10 (NASB) says, "For we are His workmanship, created in Christ Jesus for good works, which God prepared beforehand so that we would walk in them."

God was a craftsman—you are his workmanship. You are a tool in his hand. Are you walking in the good WORK that he has called you to do? Have you EMBRACED who he made you to be? Are you developing your talent? Are you increasing? Are you listening to the Holy Spirit?

I'm uncertain where I heard this phrase, but it says so much:

Let us be living epistles, written by the Holy Spirit, and read by all people.

> God was a craftsman—you are his workmanship. You are a tool in his hand. Are you walking in the good WORK that he has called you to do?

My hope is you will never again view your work, vocation, career, or calling in the marketplace as ordinary or normal. My desire is you will embrace it. My prayer is you will receive fresh insight and energy as to how you can use your skill and use "what's in your hand," and BE A CRAFTSMAN FOR GOD!

Proverbs 22:29 (NASB):
"Do you see a person skilled in his work?
He will stand before kings;
He will not stand before obscure people."

ENDNOTES

1   Robby Galatty, *"The Forgotten Jesus part 2: Was Jesus a Carpenter or a Stonemason?" Lifeway Leadership.* *https://leadership.lifeway.com/2017/04/04/the-forgotten-jesus-part-2-was-jesus-a-carpenter-or-a-stonemason/*

2   Phillip J Swanson. "Occupations and Professions of the Bible," *Holman Bible Dictionary: https://www.studylight.org/dictionaries/eng/hbd/o/occupations-and-professions-in-the-bible.html*

3   Victor H. Matthews, "Commerce," *Holman Bible Dictionary: https://www.studylight.org/dictionaries/eng/hbd/c/commerce.html*

4   Arthur Miller, *Why You Can't Be Anything You Want To Be*

5   "What does yoke mean in the Bible?" GotQuestions: https://www.gotquestions.org/yoke-in-the-Bible.html

6   "Bezalel Academy of Arts and Design." Wikipedia. Last updated July 5, 2021. https://en.wikipedia.org/wiki/Bezalel_Academy_of_Arts_and_Design

7   Russel H. Conwell. "Acres of Diamonds." *Success Classics: http://www.butler-bowdon.com/russell-h-conwell---acres-of-diamonds.html*

8   Ben Cerullo. "What's That in Your Hand?" *Inspiration.org: https://inspiration.org/christian-articles/whats-that-in-your-hand*

9   Arnold K. Garr, Christopher Columbus A Latter-Day Saint Perspective, (Provo, Utah: Religious Studies Center, Brigham Young University, 1992), 39-52. Accessed at https://rsc.byu.edu/christopher-columbus-latter-day-saint-perspective/first-voyage-americas-columbus-guided-spirit

RESOURCES

RESOURCES AND BOOKS RELATED TO THIS TOPIC
Why You Can't Be Anything You Want To Be by Arthur Miller
Supernatural Business by Mike Rovner
X: Multiply Your God-Given Potential by John Bevere
The Holy Spirit by John Bevere
Power Points for Increase by Bob Harrison
The Power to Create by Tim Redmond
Money, Truth & Life by Judy Copenbarger
Increasing Your Personal Capacity by Eddie Windsor

ASSESSMENT TESTS AND RESOURCES
The Myers & Briggs Foundation: https://www.myersbriggs.org/
The Enneagram Institute: https://www.enneagraminstitute.com/
What Color is Your Parachute: https://www.parachutebook.com/
The Balance Careers: https://www.thebalancecareers.com/
free-career-aptitude-tests-2059813
Your One Degree, by Dave Jewitt: https://www.youronedegree.com/
Integrus Leadership & The Flippen Group: https://www.integrus.org/

For more information about Mark Chapman
or to download a free

God's Craftsman Study Guide

Please visit our website:

www.godscraftsman.org

Made in the USA
Middletown, DE
03 June 2022

66563886R00071